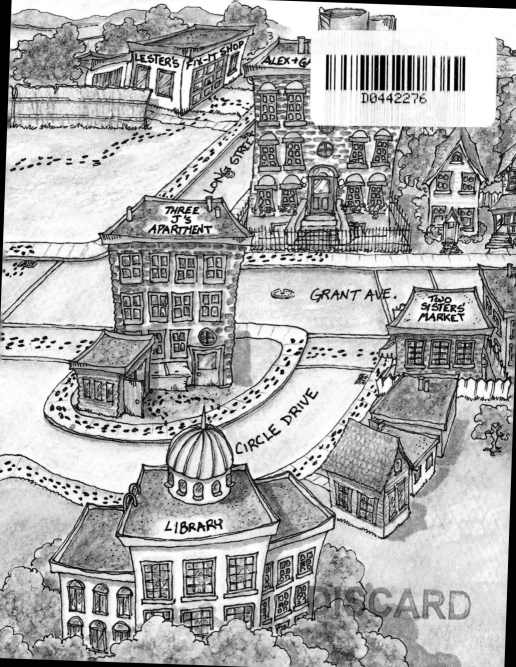

Rookie
choices®

THE BIRTHDAY FLOWERS

THE
CORNER
KIDS

Written by Larry Dane Brimner • Illustrated by Christine Tripp

Children's Press®
A Division of Scholastic Inc.
New York • Toronto • London • Auckland • Sydney
Mexico City • New Delhi • Hong Kong
Danbury, Connecticut

For "The Gardener"
—L.D.B.

For Lois Hayden, a wonderful neighbor
and my faithful supporter.
—C.T.

Reading Consultants
Linda Cornwell
Literacy Specialist

Katharine A. Kane
Education Consultant
(Retired, San Diego County Office of Education and San Diego State University)

Library of Congress Cataloging-in-Publication Data

Brimner, Larry Dane.
 The birthday flowers / Larry Dane Brimner; illustrated by Christine Tripp.
 p.cm.—(rookie choices)
 Summary: Alex, one of the Corner Kids, doesn't have enough money to buy a special bunch
of flowers for his mother, and so he takes some from the window box at Gertie's Spinning
Wheel Bike Shop instead.
 ISBN 0-516-22540-5 (lib. bdg.)   0-516-27390-6 (pbk.)
 [1. Stealing—Fiction. 2.Flowers—Fiction. 3. Conduct of life—Fiction.] I. Tripp, Christine, ill.
II. Title. III. Series
 PZ7.B767 Bm 2002
 [E]—dc21

                                        2001004946

This book is about
respect for property.

Alex looked at the bunches of flowers. They all cost more money than he had.

"May I help you?" Flora asked.

FLORA'S
FLOWER
FIELD!

Alex shrugged. "I want a bunch of flowers for my mom's birthday, but this is all I have," he said.

He pulled some coins out of his pocket.

"Forty-eight cents," said Flora. She tapped one finger against her cheek. "How about this pretty daisy?"

One daisy was not a bunch.
Alex shook his head and walked on.

11

Along the way, he passed the Spinning Wheel Bike Shop. He peeked in the window. When he did, something tickled his nose. He stepped back. Flowers spilled over the window boxes. They were beautiful.

Later that morning, the Corner Kids were making birthday cards in Alex's bedroom. Alex and his friends Gabby and Three J called themselves the Corner Kids because they lived on corners of the same street.

"What else are you giving your mom?" Gabby asked.

Alex opened his closet.

"Wow!" said Three J.
"I've never seen so many flowers."

17

"They look almost like the ones that Gertie grows in the window boxes at the bike shop," said Gabby. "She grows them for a friend of hers who can't go outside anymore."

Alex looked at the flowers.
He never thought about them
belonging to someone. He never
thought that someone might have
a plan for them.

21

"You guys wait here," he said. "I have to do something."

At the bike shop, Alex went to the counter. "These are yours," he said quietly. He gave the flowers to Gertie. "I'm sorry I picked them without asking."

It was a hard thing to say.

Gertie closed her eyes. She smelled the flowers' sweet scent. "I was afraid I wouldn't have any for my friend Mr. Short," she said. "These will make him so happy."

Alex knew they would.

On the way home, he stopped at Flora's Flower Field. The daisy was still there. Flora was right. It *was* pretty.

Later that day, the Corner Kids surprised Alex's mom. When Alex saw her smile, he knew one daisy could bring as much happiness as a room full of flowers.

ABOUT THE AUTHOR

Larry Dane Brimner studied literature and writing at San Diego State University and taught school for twenty years. The author of more than seventy-five books for children, many of them Children's Press titles, he enjoys meeting young readers and writers when he isn't at his computer.

ABOUT THE ILLUSTRATOR

Christine Tripp lives in Ottawa, Canada, with her husband Don; four grown children—Elizabeth, Erin, Emily, and Eric; son-in-law Jason; grandsons Brandon and Kobe; four cats; and one very large, scruffy puppy named Jake.